Marshmallows

Victoria Blakemore

For Ms. B because... marshmallows!

© 2017 Victoria Blakemore

All rights reserved. This book or parts thereof may not be reproduced in any form, stored in any retrieval system, or transmitted in any form by any means—electronic, mechanical, photocopy, recording, or otherwise—without prior written permission of the publisher, except as provided by United States of America copyright law. For permission requests, write to the publisher, at "Attention: Permissions Coordinator," at the address below.

vblakemore.author@gmail.com

Copyright info/picture credits

Cover, Irina Burakova/AdobeStock; Page 3, StockSnap/Pixabay; Page 5, pixel2013/Pixabay; Page 7, lesichkadesign/AdobeStock; Page 9, JACLOU-DL/Pixabay; Page 11, panor156/AdobeStock; Page 13, Mark S/flickr; Page 15, AnnBehemotik/Pixabay; Page 17, gwgladstone/Pixabay; Page 19, Storyblocks; Page 21, TerriC/Pixabay; Page 23; Alexas_Fotos/Pixabay; Page 25, Joy/flickr; Page 27, Irina Burakova/AdobeStock; Page 29, flockine/Pixabay; Page 31, Daryl Musser/AdobeStock; Page 33, svetlana_cherruty/AdobeStock

Table of Contents

What are Marshmallows?	2
Ingredients	4
Mallow Plant	6
History	8
Production	12
Toasted Marshmallows	14
S'mores	16
Hot Cocoa	18
Easter Treats	20
Marshmallow Candies	22
Marshmallow Crème	24
Popularity	26
Nutrition	28
Recipes	30
Glossary	34

What Are Marshmallows?

Marshmallows are soft, fluffy sweets. They are a common addition to many different recipes.

While many people think of marshmallows as white and round, they can be made in many different shapes and colors.

Ingredients

Marshmallows used to be made with sap from the mallow plant, egg whites, and sugar. It took a long time to make them.

Now, marshmallows are made with gelatin, sugar, water, starch, and corn syrup. They are much faster and easier to make now.

The gelatin in marshmallows is what makes them soft and spongy. It helps keep them fresh longer.

Mallow Plants

There are nearly thirty kinds of mallow plants. Parts of them are **edible**. Mallow leaves and flowers are sometimes used in salads.

The marshmallow plant is a kind of mallow plant. They are found around marshes, which is how they got their name.

Marshmallows were first made with a sap taken from the roots of the marshmallow plant.

History

The first marshmallows were made by ancient Egyptians thousands of years ago. They were considered a **delicacy** and eaten mainly by royalty.

The marshmallows made by the Egyptians were made from sap from mallow roots. The sap was mixed with nuts and honey.

A mixture made with parts of the mallow plant can help with cough, sore throat, upset stomach, and toothache.

The food we think of as marshmallows today was first made in France in the 1800's. Candy makers mixed the mallow sap with egg whites and corn syrup.

The result was a gooey sweet that could be molded into different shapes.

Marshmallows were often sold **individually** as candies in candy shops.

Production

The process for making marshmallows has changed a lot over time. It used to take more than a day for a marshmallow to be made.

Marshmallows had to be put into molds to give them their shape. It would take time for them to set.

Since the 1950's, marshmallows have been made using special tubes. Now it only takes a few minutes.

Toasted Marshmallows

Marshmallows are very popular camping treats. They are often toasted over a campfire.

When marshmallows are held over a heat source, the outside toasts. The inside melts and becomes gooey.

The outside of a toasted marshmallow is golden-brown in color. If it catches on fire, it may be black.

S'mores

In 1927, the first recipe for s'mores was published in the Girl Scouts Handbook. The name means "some more" because people usually want more than one!

S'mores are made with toasted marshmallows, graham crackers, and chocolate.

Toasted marshmallows are put together with a chocolate bar in between two graham crackers. The heat from the marshmallows melts the chocolate.

Hot Cocoa

Hot cocoa is made in the winter as a sweet way to warm up when it is cold outside.

Marshmallows are often added to hot cocoa. The heat from the drink melts the marshmallows, adding extra sweetness to the drink.

Easter Treats

Some of the most popular Easter treats are marshmallow chicks and bunnies. Once they are shaped, they are rolled in colored sugar.

These sweet treats used to be made completely by hand. There are now machines that can make them more quickly.

It used to take about twenty-seven hours to make one marshmallow chick or bunny. Now, it takes about six minutes.

Marshmallow Candies

Marshmallows are often used in candy-making because of their sweet taste.

When making candies, some people like to make their marshmallows from scratch. Then, they can add chocolate, colored sugar, or sprinkles.

Chocolate-dipped marshmallows are a quick and easy treat to make. They can also be covered in chocolate and sprinkles.

Marshmallow Crème

Marshmallow crème is made with many of the same ingredients as marshmallows. The main difference is the use of egg whites instead of gelatin.

This is why marshmallow crème doesn't hold a shape and can be easily spread.

Marshmallow crème can be used as a frosting or filling for baked goods. Some people make sandwiches with marshmallow crème and peanut butter.

Popularity

Marshmallows are made and sold all over the world. People in the United States buy more marshmallows than any other country.

It has been **estimated** that over ninety million pounds of marshmallows are bought in a year in America.

Most marshmallows are sold between the months of October and December.

Nutrition

Marshmallows are filled with sugar, so they are very sweet. There are other snacks that are healthier.

Eating too much sugar can make you feel like you have lots of energy, but that feeling wears off. Then you can feel very tired.

Marshmallows are very sugary.

They should be eaten in

moderation.

Recipes

Peanut Butter Marshmallow Sandwich

Ingredients:

Marshmallow crème   2 slices of bread

Peanut butter

Directions:

1. Spread peanut butter on one piece of bread.

2. Spread marshmallow crème on the other slice of bread.

3. Put the two slices together and enjoy!

Substitute crackers for the bread to make a quick, sweet snack!

Marshmallow Pops

Ingredients:

Marshmallows   Lollipop sticks

Melted milk or white chocolate

Colored sugar or sprinkles

Directions:

1. Spear marshmallow with lollipop stick, being careful not to go all the way through.
2. Dip the marshmallow into the melted chocolate.
3. Roll the marshmallow in colored sugar or sprinkles

Try different combinations of chocolate and sprinkles. Once the chocolate hardens, cover the marshmallows with lollipop bags to keep fresh.

Glossary

Delicacy: something rare and special

Edible: able to be safely eaten

Estimated: when a careful guess is made about size or amount

Individually: one by one, one at a time

Moderation: not having too much

Substitution: using something in place of something else

About the Author

Victoria Blakemore is a first grade teacher in Southwest Florida with a passion for reading.

You can visit her at

www.elementaryexplorers.com

Also in This Series

Also in This Series

www.ingramcontent.com/pod-product-compliance
Lightning Source LLC
Chambersburg PA
CBHW042000080526
44588CB00021B/2815